Perfectly FLAWED

God Transforms Our Weaknesses into Strengths

LEADER GUIDE

LISA TONEY

Abingdon Women | Nashville

Perfectly Flawed
God Transforms Our Weaknesses into Strengths
Leader Guide

Copyright © 2025 Abingdon Press
All rights reserved.

ISBN: 978-17910-3256-2

MANUFACTURED IN THE UNITED STATES OF AMERICA

Contents

About the Author

Hello, I'm Lisa.

"For **THIS,** we have Jesus."

This is my battle cry. In every situation, it seems to apply. Jesus makes all the difference in the world.

Every morning, I am shocked, overjoyed, humbled, and bursting with gratitude. Out of this overflow, I love to speak and write about ways to build easy, intentional, and powerful faith habits to live for Jesus. As a professor and pastor, I love to help people answer the "why" behind the faith habits I teach.

I've listened, learned, taught, and served alongside the church for more than twenty years. As the CEO of Faith Habits, my joy is to provide faith-based classes, coaching, and resources to encourage engagement with God.

With a master's in divinity from Fuller Theological Seminary and a communications degree from Taylor University, my passions are faith and communication. Partnering with Women of Faith, Aspire Women's Events, and Guideposts are some of the super fun opportunities God has brought my way.

In addition to this study, I have authored the projects *Thrive: Live Like You Matter, The Scripture Challenge,* and *The Wholehearted Psalms Devotion Series.*

After growing up in the Midwest, I discovered I'm solar-powered and now live in Southern California with my husband, four kids, a puppy, a gecko, and five chickens. My husband and I often lead faith-based group tours of the Bible lands (Israel, Greece, Italy, Turkey, etc.) with InspireTravelGroup.org and walk where the unstoppable, incomparable, life-changing movement of Jesus began.

Let's be friends!

[Instagram] LisaToneyLife

[Facebook] LisaToneyLife

[YouTube] Lisa Toney

[WWW] lisatoney.com

Introduction

Welcome to *Perfectly Flawed*. I'm so glad that you have picked up this leader guide that goes along with the participant workbook and videos. If you are leading a group, this is full of resources for you to help equip you and prepare you to facilitate.

Right off the bat, let me say thank you for your willingness to lead a group. Whether you are an experienced group leader or a newbie, leading takes some extra time to prepare, pray, and put into practice a group experience.

Gathering a Group

Wouldn't you love spending time each week with some of your closest friends? I love to be invited to things, don't you? Even if I can't go, I love being asked. It makes me feel valued and included. Although many of us lead exceptionally complicated lives, we can sometimes feel lonely as we are caught up in our busy, overwhelming schedules. Being in someone's thoughts is a blessing.

I bet if you reach out and invite ten women to join you for a Bible study, you'll probably get at least six who would be excited to join you, and just like that, you've got an amazing community to share your life and talk about your faith for the next six weeks.

We need more friends in our lives. We need more of Jesus. This gives you a win-win!

Let's encourage women to connect, share their lives, get intentional with Jesus, pray together, and have a lot of fun doing it!

List at least ten people you would like to do this study with. If you can think of more than that, include them. When it comes to loving one another and learning more about Jesus, the more the merrier!

Although each lesson in the participant's workbook offers insight and background into the Scripture passages, don't skip over reading the passages themselves. The best way to study the Bible is to read the Bible. This study will walk you and your group through different passages

and help you slow your roll. Sometimes I can read over a portion of Scripture and not absorb it. I'm going too fast; I get distracted. The other participants in the group may feel the same. Scripture is not always easy to read, and it can be quite tempting to indulge in TL;DR—too long; didn't read!

I know we are all busy. I am with you there! Life never seems to stop. With that said, sometimes we are just in a space where it is hard to add one more thing. I get it. I've been in all those places, but choosing to be intentional in growing closer to Jesus amid busyness could be the *best* thing for you. Acknowledge to your group that you understand this and are excited that they are taking this time to grow closer to God. Encourage them to take their time in their private study and absorb all that God is telling them or leading them to.

Let me be so bold as to say, it's a *game-changer.*

Here's a sample text you can use to invite people to join you.

> Hey friend! I am putting together a little group for the next six weeks to do a Bible study. 📖 🙏 🤍 ✝️
>
> It's going to be so fun. 💃 😎 🙋 It's all about how God can use us in spite of our flaws! 💯
>
> I need that encouragement; how about you? We are going to meet on (insert day) at this time (insert time) starting on (insert start date) at (insert location). ☑️ 👍
>
> Can you join us? I'm bringing (insert fav food)! I'm excited to spend time with you and hear your heart. 🤍 🥰

About the Participant Workbook

The participant workbook for this study will guide the women in your group through a daily time with God, during which they will engage His Word and allow Him to speak to their hearts through the disciple Peter and his relationship with Jesus. Before the first session, make sure each member of your group has a copy, and encourage them to complete the first week of readings before the first group session.

Each week features five devotional lessons that include both Scripture study as well as reflection, worship, and prayer. Encourage the women in your group to find a quiet place—maybe a favorite chair or a spot on the front porch or back deck—where they can spend their devotional time with Peter and Jesus.

Each week begins with "A Word from Peter," which provides a brief insight into the life of the disciple and carries participants a little deeper into his world. Then, each day begins with the focus verse of the week, followed by stories from Scripture and questions that will guide the participants into thoughts and reflections on what they've learned from the readings. Each day's lesson also includes a QR code, which participant can use a smart phone to link to a YouTube video to aid in their worship time.

On average, the lessons can be completed in about twenty to thirty minutes—depending on how much time the women spend in reflection on the questions. Completing these readings each week will prepare them for the discussion and activities in the group session.

About This Leader Guide

This leader guide will provide suggestions and support for facilitating each group session. It is written so that you do not have to be a professional or experienced teacher to do this! For instance, any repetition in the suggestions is for focus, so you do not need to review the previous week's ideas. All you really need is a desire for a deeper relationship with God and other believers, and a willingness to not only share your own faith and struggles with the group but to also encourage them to do the same. Between this guide and the participant's workbook, you have everything you need to lead a beneficial gathering of women who want to develop a closer relationship with the Lord—and one another!

As you gather each week with the members of your group, you will have the opportunity to watch a video related to the study, discuss the questions and reflections from each day's lessons, respond to what you're learning, and worship and pray together. You will need access to a television and a DVD player. If you prefer, you may access the videos for this study (and other Abingdon Women Bible studies) on AmplifyMedia.com through a subscription. Whatever you're comfortable with!

Creating a warm and inviting atmosphere will help to make the women feel welcome. Although optional, you might provide snacks and drinks for your first meeting. During the introduction time, invite group members to rotate in bringing refreshments each week. This encourages women to show off their own gifts of hospitality and contribute to the group.

Group Leader Resources

This leader guide and the DVD/video files will be your primary tools for leading each group session. In this book, you will find outlines for six group sessions, each formatted for either 60 or 90 minutes:

60-MINUTE FORMAT

Leader Prep (Before the Session)

Welcome and Opening Prayer	5 minutes
Icebreaker	5 minutes
Video	20–25 minutes
Group Discussion and Worship	20–25 minutes
Closing Prayer	5 minutes

90-MINUTE FORMAT

Leader Prep (Before the Session)

Welcome and Opening Prayer	5–10 minutes
Icebreaker	5 minutes
Video	20–25 minutes
Group Discussion	30–35 minutes
Deeper Conversation and Worship	15 minutes
Closing Prayer	5 minutes

As you can see, the 90-minute format is identical to the 60-minute format but has more time for welcoming/fellowship and group discussion, plus a deeper conversation exercise for small groups. Or your group might prefer to limit the welcome time and extend the closing prayer time. If your discussion has been lively, use the worship time to bring everyone back together with a focus on Jesus.

For the Leader Prep time, it is helpful to meet 30–60 minutes before the group arrives so that your group facilitators have an opportunity to share with one another what God has been doing in their own hearts and lives. This is also a wonderful opportunity to pray together specifically for that day and group discussions. There will be some sweet moments of sharing God's mighty work of healing, hope, and transformation.

Group Facilitators

Keep in mind that every group is different. If you lead more than one group through this study (or have led a group before), you'll discover that the flow of each group will depend on its members. Some women will feel freer to share thoughts and observations; others will be reluctant for any number of reasons. Each comment offered can spark different levels of discussions. Adapt the format, individual segments, and activities to meet the specific needs and preferences of your group.

Leadership Tips

Prior to the first meeting, communicate the importance of completing the weekly devotional lessons and participating in group discussion. Each participant needs to bring their participant's workbook and Bible to the sessions. Have a few extra Bibles handy for those who may not have their own—or have forgotten it for the session.

Arrive early for each session to make sure the room and equipment are prepared. Take a moment to pray alone for the session and each participant.

Personally welcome and greet each person. You might want to have a sign-up list before or at the first meeting for the women to record their names and preferred contact information.

At the start of each session, ask the participants to turn off or silence their cell phones (or eliminate other distractions if meeting online).

Always start on time. Honor the time of those who are punctual.

Encourage everyone to participate fully but don't put anyone on the spot. Don't rush to fill the silence but be prepared to offer a personal example or answer if no one else responds at first. Remind them that this is a time of trust, and whatever is discussed during the session should never be shared with others. Facilitate but don't dominate. If you talk most of the time, group members may tend to listen rather than engage. Your task is to encourage conversation and keep the discussion moving.

If someone monopolizes the conversation, kindly thank her for sharing and ask if anyone else has any insights or move on to the next discussion point. Keep an eye on the clock and try not to let anyone rule any discussion. Once the sharing starts and the women become more comfortable and open with one another, letting the time run long will be an easy temptation. But we are all busy! Try to honor everyone's time and commitment.

Try not to interrupt, judge, or minimize anyone's comments or input.

You are not expected to be the expert or have all the answers. Acknowledge that all of you are on this journey together, with the Holy Spirit as your leader and guide. If issues or questions arise that you don't feel equipped to handle or answer, make a note and talk with the pastor or a staff member at your church. After you have a more complete answer, circle back to the topic—briefly!—at the beginning of the next session.

End on time. If you are running over, give members the opportunity to leave if they need to. Don't rush but wrap up as quickly as you can with prayer requests and the closing prayer. Thank them for coming and let them know you're looking forward to seeing them next time.

Be prepared for some who want to hang out and talk at the end. If you need everyone to leave by a certain time, communicate this at the beginning of the group session. If you are meeting in a church during regularly scheduled activities, be aware of childcare closing times.

Leader Preparation Before the Session

Intended to aid your preparation prior to the group session, this section provides an overview of the week's Bible story and theme, the main point of the session, key scriptures, and a list of materials and equipment needed. Be sure to review this section, as well as the session outline, to plan and prepare before the group meets. You also may find it helpful to watch the video segments in advance so you are familiar with the content. View the YouTube video(s) linked in the lessons, because questions may arise (especially the first week) regarding content or how they should be used. Each study day has a worship song linked by a QR code that the women can utilize to have a space to worship.

WELCOME AND OPENING PRAYER

To create a warm, welcoming environment as the women arrive, consider either providing coffee, tea, or other refreshments, or playing worship music, or both. Candles can also create a warm atmosphere but note any restrictions at your meeting place regarding candles (if not meeting at your home) and be aware of possible sensitivities to perfumes or other scented items. Be sure to provide name tags if the women do not know one another or you have new participants in your group. Then, when you are ready to begin, pray the opening prayer that is provided or offer your own.

ICEBREAKER

Use the icebreaker to briefly engage the women in the topic while helping them feel comfortable with one another.

VIDEO

Next, watch the week's video segment together. Be sure to direct participants to each week's "Learn with Lisa: Video Viewer Guide" in the participant workbook, which they may complete as they watch the video. Answers can be found in both the participant workbook (page 232) and this leader guide (page 60).

GROUP DISCUSSION AND WORSHIP

After watching the video, choose from the questions provided to facilitate group discussion over both the video and the participant workbook. More questions are provided than you will have time to include. Before the session, select important points from the lesson that you want to cover, putting a check mark beside them in your book. Reflect on each question and make some notes in the margins to share during your discussion time. Participants will need Bibles to look up various supplementary Scriptures.

Depending on the number of women in your group and the level of their participation, you may not have time to cover everything you have selected, and that is okay. Rather than attempting to bulldoze through, follow the Spirit's lead and be open to where the Spirit takes the conversation. Remember that your role is not to have all the answers but to encourage discussion and sharing.

To conclude the discussion, use a suggested worship video from the week's lessons to bring the women back together. Encourage them to prayerfully listen to the lyrics and reflect on how the song impacts their own thoughts about the discussion.

Deeper Conversation

If your group is meeting for 90 minutes, move to this exercise for deeper sharing. This leader's guide contains questions for this deeper conversation, which allows women to share more intimately and build connections with one another. Also, allow the participants to ask questions that are on their hearts or minds, but be mindful to guide the discussion so it does not go too far off topic.

If you have a large group (ten to twelve or more), consider breaking into small groups of three or four for this time for more intimate discussions, but allow time to bring everyone back together for summary statements and concluding thoughts.

If you utilize the 90-minute format, hold the worship time at the end so you can recenter the group on the study and their own reflections.

Closing Prayer

Close by leading the group in prayer. Invite the women to name prayer requests briefly. To get things started, you might share a personal request of your own. As women share their requests, model for the group by writing each request in your participant workbook, indicating that you will remember to pray for them during the week.

As the study progresses, you might encourage members to participate in the Closing Prayer by praying out loud for one another and the requests given. Ask the women to volunteer to pray for specific requests or direct each woman to pray for the person on her right or left. If you are using name tags, make sure they are visible so that group members do not feel awkward if they do not remember someone's name.

After the prayer, remind the women to pray for one another throughout the week.

Leader Questions and Suggestions

If this is a church-based study group, how long should I promote it before starting?

Promotion should be launched and going strong at least three to four weeks before the group study begins. If you are in a larger church, you'll want to talk with the communications team about their recommendations for a marketing timeline for the study. Also ask if the study can be promoted on social media, the church's website, in the worship service, in a targeted email, or other churchwide communications. This gets it on people's calendars and allows them time to get signed up and invite friends! Advertise early. You need to get the word out to give people enough time to plan to join you! You can access easy-peasy promotion materials at lisatoney.com/perfectlyflawedresources.

If this is a small group in your home or other private setting, send out the invitations at least a month before starting, and encourage people to RSVP two weeks before the start date. One week before starting, send reminders to those who wish to join you. Send another the day before beginning. If participants are being asked to provide their own workbook, include purchasing information or links with each contact.

How big should our groups be?

This study works with a small group gathered around a dining room table, sitting in a living room, or hanging out at a cafe. A large group can gather at your church or community center. If you have a larger group, discussion is most effective if you enlist discussion facilitators who can lead and ask questions in a small group. You can pick the group size that works around the size of your tables, but I recommend six to ten in each group.

How should I get organized to lead this study?

It's always more fun with a team! If you anticipate a large crowd from your church or neighborhood, enlist a few friends to help with one specific aspect of the Bible study. Here are some ideas (you can mix and match or change based on your context):

1. Team Lead: Oversees all team positions and leads group facilitators
2. Marketing Maestro: Champions all things promotion
3. Hospitality Host: Snack attack and coffee consumption master planner
4. Prayer Warrior: Intercession advocate and manager of prayer requests

5. Décor Queen: Make it memorable! Create inspired spaces for your group.
6. Registration Rockstar: Sign-ups, book distribution, money collection, weekly attendance
7. Service Project Coordinator: How can our group *Be the Light* in our community?
8. Welcome Wagon: Greet, hug, high-five, smile, and create a warm environment.
9. Setup Lead: Get all the things out.
10. Teardown Lead: Put all the things away.
11. Childcare Lead: Create, champion, and oversee a plan for childcare.
12. Worship Lead: Oversee the worship time for the group gathering.

How long is the study?

While intended as a six-week study, some groups may want to add an optional seventh week as a launch week or an introductory session. The two options are outlined below:

1. **Six Weeks**: Week 1 must be completed before the first group gathering. This requires participants to have their books in advance, either through their own purchase or distributed in some fashion prior to the first session. This may be more difficult if some of the participants have not taken part in a study like this before, or if they are not part of an established group, such as a church or community center. In this layout, participants *must* complete the first session on their own.
2. **Seven Weeks**: This week can be a launch with just a short meeting to hand out study books, assign small groups, cast a vision for the study, and provide time for fellowship. However, there is an introductory video session available for use. If you choose to use it, you will need to allocate 15–20 minutes to view it. You can download the video at lisatoney.com/perfectlyflawedresources.

Should we offer childcare?

This will depend on the group participating. If you have parents of young children or homeschooling families who are participants (or you want them to participate), this will be ***essential***. There are many ways that groups navigate this. It can be done!

1. If your church offers childcare during set hours, see if you can offer this Bible study to parallel those times. Collaborate with the children's ministry leader(s) and see if they can work with your group.
2. Recruit volunteer babysitters. Perhaps some high school or college students in your community would enjoy providing childcare as volunteer service hours.

3. Hire babysitters. Some groups build the cost for childcare providers into the price of the study.

4. If you are doing this Bible study in a home, find a game to play or a great movie for the kids to watch while the adults gather for their study and discussion.

What are some decoration ideas if I like to theme it up?

Oh yeah. I love that you are leaning in. Centerpieces or stage backdrops can be a lot of fun. Since Peter was a fisherman, you can do many easy things to add a fun ambiance to this study. Here are some ideas to get your juices flowing: fishing nets, shells, sand, water, wooden boats, oars, and so forth. You can also draw on the *Perfectly Flawed* theme and work with broken things that are also beautiful: cracked mirrors, broken pots, and so forth.

Do you have some fun swag we can sport?

Sure do! Grab some fun t-shirts, bags, stickers, and other fun goodies to REPRESENT at lisatoney.com/perfectlyflawedresources.

What service projects could we do that relate to this study?

Love this! Let's put our faith into practice. One easy service project is to collect cans of tuna, salmon, and canned seafood (Get it? Peter was a fisherman!) for food pantries. Food banks usually run low on proteins, and this can be a massive blessing for families.

If your church has a missions or outreach team, ask them for suggestions. They may already have connections with local organizations. Even if they do not, there are tons of great organizations with which to partner. Pray and ask the Holy Spirit to lead the way in giving an idea to your group! Signing up to serve outside the study provides an incredible bonding opportunity and pushes us to sacrifice our time to serve others. Volunteering with a local organization in your community is something I always encourage. It is a great way to be the hands and feet of Jesus and shine His light in our communities. I recommend setting this as a group expectation at the beginning of the study and doing your service experience after Week 4 is completed.

If I'm planning a larger group, how should I recruit group facilitators?

Start with those you know who are fun, kind, compassionate, timely, and have spiritual maturity. Invite them to be group facilitators. You want people who can interact with various personalities and spiritual maturity levels. Group facilitator guidelines are provided so that you can train your team. Another option is to invite people to become group facilitators during the registration period. If you choose to do this, include the expectations and a screening process. This can be done with either an application or a conversation, or both—either in person or by phone—to ensure you feel they can commit and represent your group well. Provide an overview of the study and walk through the format so they feel comfortable. They should understand and be able to explain to their groups how the study will work.

Meet with group facilitators either online or in person one week before you start the study to ensure you have set them up for success by equipping and encouraging them.

Group Facilitators Guidelines

Names are important. *Get in the game; remember their name.*

Encourage your group facilitators to learn the names of their group members as quickly as possible. I'm a big fan of name tags every week, so we can all look one another in the eye and call one another by name. This helps everyone feel seen and known!

Trust is essential. *Lock it down; don't spread it around.*

If groups do not keep their discussions private, there is no trust. Your group facilitator(s) should emphasize this each week (with the caveat of danger or abuse to self or others; this may require outside help). Confidentiality allows everyone to feel safe and free to be honest without the fear it will end up on social media, included on a church prayer list, or shared with someone who is not safe. Encourage group facilitators to talk with you if they hear or see something beyond their comfort level. *Who should they go to if someone in their group needs immediate intervention or crisis care?*

Time management is valuable. *Be prompt; it's what we want.*

Start on time. End on time. Monitor each section of the lesson for timeliness and group participation. Small group facilitators should get there early for the team huddle and to be ready to greet their group members warmly. If an important discussion goes later than the set time, give permission to those who need to leave on time. Everyone feels respected when their time is honored. Encourage group members to share for a few minutes so that everyone gets a turn. If a group has a challenge with this, a facilitator can use a timer or have permission to interrupt graciously. Sample: *Sue, we love hearing from you, but we want to let everyone have a turn to share. Go ahead and finish up (land the plane) so we can hear from Jen too.*

Facilitators set the tone. *Show the way that vulnerability is okay.*

No one needs to discuss anything that they are uncomfortable sharing. Especially during the first week or two, women who may never have participated in a group like this may not be comfortable with trusting others yet. Modeling honesty is helpful for others to know how to do so as well. If some group members are quiet, a facilitator can ask them by name, saying something like, "Pam, I'd love to hear your perspective." Sometimes, people won't respond unless they are asked. However, group members should feel free to "pass" if they are uncomfortable sharing.

Everyone's voice matters. *Experience grace in our discussion space!*

This is a Bible study, so there is homework! This is always a challenging aspect to navigate. Some groups prefer you to have your homework done before you participate in the discussion, while other groups want everyone to come regardless of how much homework they completed. You'll have to decide what will work best in your context. Each week's discussion guide follows the video teaching, so there is space for interaction with the video teaching and the homework. If you think some people may have trouble completing all the work, be prepared to point out questions from the next week's lessons that you plan to discuss. This allows women to focus on those if they have a harried schedule.

Pray for your group. *When in doubt, pray it out!*

If you ever get to a difficult place in your group discussion and you aren't sure what to do or how to transition, **stop and pray for that person**. This study is a vital part of the group's bonding, but nothing should outweigh the need to stop and pray for a friend who is struggling. It is a powerful way to help them by entrusting their heart to God. It is also helpful to provide a transition to the next discussion question.

The closing prayer is a great way to end your time together after the discussion. You can handle prayer requests in a variety of ways. You can use the space in your workbook to write down prayer requests, use an index card to write them down, use a prayer app, or have one person record requests. You can easily take a photo of the page of requests and text or email it to your group. The group facilitator should plan to close the group in prayer for the first week. After that, encourage prayer participation with an invitation for someone else to pray or by doing "popcorn" prayer (simple, one-sentence prayers offered by anyone in the group).

Throw a lot of kindness confetti. *In the company of friends, loneliness ends!*

Loneliness is an epidemic that we as believers want to eliminate. Connections with real, live humans are life-giving. Have fun, be yourself, and encourage others as much as you can. Amazing things happen when people feel seen, heard, known, and loved. Be a friendship architect by helping those in your group build bridges with one another. You have the privilege of encouraging friendships to grow! Make it clear to each woman that she is greatly appreciated, loved, and prayed for.

Would Your Group Love a Visit from Lisa?

As pastor, teacher, author, and professor, Lisa loves to connect with other women studying the Bible and exploring faith. She offers a virtual, fifteen-minute drop-in visit for groups of twenty-five participants or more who are studying *Perfectly Flawed*. (*Visits based on author availability.*)

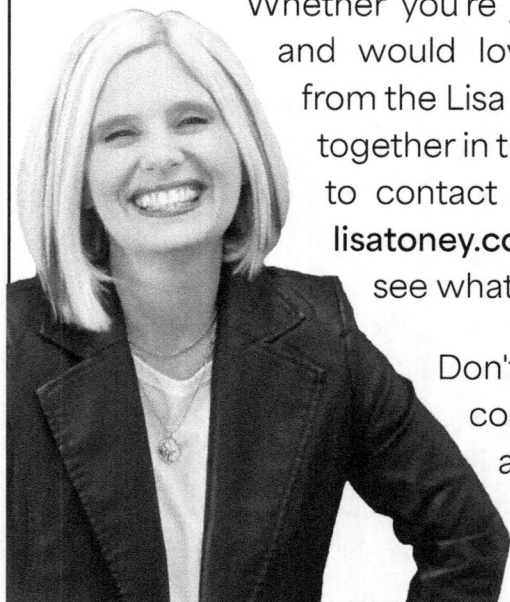

Whether you're just starting the first session and would love some inspiration straight from the Lisa or you've spent several weeks together in this experience, Lisa invites you to contact her directly at **https://www.lisatoney.com/perfectlyflaweddropin** to see what can be arranged!

Don't miss this opportunity to connect with an inspiring author and to discover what it means to be a flawed but faithful servant!

Perfectly FLAWED

and

CHOSEN

(Peter Met Jesus)

Notes

Leader Preparation (Before the Session)

Overview

This week, we looked at selected verses from the life of Peter, including selections from his epistles (1–2 Peter), Acts, and the Gospels. This week focused on his first meetings with Jesus, his choice to follow Him, and the consequences of that choice. It also focused on relationships in our own lives and how they are altered—good and bad—over time, and how new friendships can help us grow even as long-term friendships can provide support and grounding. New friendships can refresh us while old friendships can nourish us. Reread "A Word from Peter" (page 14) and think about your answers to the discussion questions.

Focus Verse

But you are a chosen people, a royal priesthood, a holy nation, God's special possession, that you may declare the praises of him who called you out of darkness into his wonderful light.

(1 Peter 2:9)

What You Will Need

- *Perfectly Flawed* DVD and DVD player, or equipment to stream the lesson-related video online
- Your Bible and your *Perfectly Flawed Participant Workbook* for reference
- Notebook or clipboard with paper for participants to sign up for either texts, emails, or both, from you or other members. Also have a sheet for snack sign-ups.
- Markerboard or chart paper and markers (optional)
- Stick-on name tags and markers (optional)
- Smartphone or tablet and a portable speaker (optional)
- Various versions of the Bible for additional references or for participants who might have forgotten theirs
- YouTube videos cued up and ready to play

Session Outline

Welcome and Opening Prayer (5-10 minutes, depending on session length)

To create a warm, welcoming environment as the women are gathering before the session begins, consider providing coffee or other refreshments and playing worship music through a Bluetooth speaker. (Have these set up and running before the participants arrive.) See the introduction for suggestions regarding décor.

Remember to greet each person individually and be sure to provide name tags if the women do not know one another or you have new participants in your group. Take note of whether they have brought the workbook and Bible with them.

You may have to do a bit of housekeeping in this first session, such as reminding them to bring the workbook and Bible. Also encourage women to sign up for bringing snacks and drinks to future meetings. Pass around a notebook (or piece of paper and a pen) for women to list contact information to be shared with the group for texts, email, calls, and so forth. If someone is uncomfortable sharing this information, do not press or make judgmental statements. The likelihood is that their reluctance will change as the sessions progress.

Allow the participants to mingle as they grab snacks, but encourage them to find their preferred seats quickly, as you plan to start on time. When you are ready to begin, pray the opening prayer that is provided below or offer your own.

Opening Prayer

Lord, we thank You for allowing us to gather to learn more about You and Your servant Peter. Open our hearts to the lessons of this study and allow us to see how You work in the lives of even the most flawed of people. We ask that You use this study to help us grow closer to You and Your son, Jesus. Amen.

Icebreaker (5 minutes)

Use the following icebreaker question to briefly engage the women and to help them feel comfortable with one another. Ask a fun light-hearted question such as, what is your favorite vacation spot and why?

Video (20-25 minutes)

Next, watch the week's video segment together. Be sure to direct participants to "Learn with Lisa: Video Viewer Guide" in the participant workbook (page 44), which they may complete as they watch the video. Some groups find it helpful to put these answers up on a slide or whiteboard before or after the teaching time to reduce the stress of some women to get all the answers right. Whatever you choose, just let your group know so that they know how to find the answers if they miss one of the fill-in-the-blanks. Lisa highlights the point on the screen during the teaching time, so most group members should be able to follow along easily. (Answers can be found on page 60 of this leader guide or page 232 of the participant workbook.)

Group Discussion (25-35 minutes, depending on session length)

After watching the video, choose from the questions provided below to facilitate group discussion. Questions are provided for both the video and the participant workbook. For the workbook portion, you may choose to read aloud excerpts from the participant workbook or express them in your own words. If reading excerpts, let participants know which page you are on so they can follow along in their books. Then use one or more of the questions that follow to guide your conversation.

Note that more material is provided than you will have time to include. Before the session, select what you want to cover, putting a check mark beside it in your book. Reflect on each question and make some notes in the margins so you can share them during your discussion time. Participants will need Bibles to look up various supplementary scriptures.

Depending on the number of women in your group and the level of their participation, you may not have time to cover everything you have selected, and that is okay. Rather than attempting to bulldoze through, follow the Spirit's lead and be open to where the Spirit takes the conversation. Remember that your role is not to have all the answers but to encourage discussion and sharing.

VIDEO DISCUSSION QUESTIONS:

- Why do you think Peter obeyed Jesus's requests to row away from the shore?
- What do you think made the relationship between Peter and Jesus unique, even among the disciples?
- What qualities do you see in Peter that made him a good leader?
- What does the phrase "living hope" mean to you?

PARTICIPANT WORKBOOK DISCUSSION QUESTIONS:

- What pet peeves do you have about others?
- What do you think about being perfectly flawed? How does that relate to how you think of yourself?
- What stands out about how Jesus connected with Peter and chose him as one of His disciples?
- Where do you need the strength of God to fill an area of weakness in your life abundantly?
- What is one thing that you would like your group to pray for you this week?

Deeper Conversation (15 minutes)

If your group is meeting for 90 minutes, you can choose to stay together for more discussion time or divide into groups of two or three within your small group. This time allows women to share more intimately and build connections with one another. (If breaking into smaller groups, encourage the women to break into different groups each week.) Before the session, write on a marker board or large piece of paper one or more of the questions below for groups to discuss. Give a two-minute warning before time is up so that the groups may wrap up their conversations.

Suggested additional questions for Week 1: (Participants may wish to refer to their participant workbooks. Page number references are provided beside each question.)

- What do you need from the power of the presence of Jesus right now? (page 19)
- What are some expectations you had for your life that have not turned out to be your reality? (page 21)
- Can you think of some ways that Jesus has shown up for you lately? Has this had any long-term effect on your life or faith? (page 29)
- Who is a teacher, mentor, or coach from whom you have learned much? What did you learn? (page 33)

Worship Time

When you sense the discussion has concluded, and especially if there is not enough time to engage in deeper, small group conversations, encourage the group take a few moments and worship the Lord who has brought you together. To guide them, play one of the YouTube videos featured this week and allow a few moments of silent reflection before you take prayer requests. You may find that worship works well to ease your group from a deep discussion into a time of prayer.

Closing Comments and Prayer (5 minutes)

Invite the women to briefly name prayer requests. To get things started, you might share a personal request of your own. As women share their requests, model for the group by writing each request in your participant workbook, indicating that you will remember to pray for them during the week.

As the study progresses, you might encourage members to participate in the Closing Prayer by praying out loud for one another and the requests given. Call on the women to pray for specific requests, or have each woman pray for the woman to her right or left. Make sure name tags are visible so that group members do not feel awkward if they do not remember someone's name.

Close by leading the group in prayer, using the written prayer below, or offer a closing prayer yourself. Afterward, remind women to pray for one another throughout the week and text at least one member this week to remind them you are praying for them and that God loves them deeply.

CLOSING PRAYER

Father, we praise Your name and offer thanks for the gifts You have bestowed on all of us. We thank You as well for giving us this time together for fellowship and growth, and we pray that as we go through this coming week, we will remember and pray for each person here. Thank You for Your work in all our lives. Amen.

Perfectly FLAWED and CALLED

(Peter Walked with Jesus)

Notes

_____

_____

_____

_____

_____

_____

_____

_____

_____

_____

Leader Preparation (Before the Session)

Overview

This week, we looked at selected verses from the life of Peter, including selections from his Epistles (1–2 Peter), Acts, and the Gospels. This week focused on his personal growth as he traveled with Jesus and listened to His teachings, especially through the parables. The lesson also focused on how stories instruct us, and how a lesson embedded in a story is easier to remember and absorb. Jesus used stories to direct His disciples and other followers, leading and encouraging them through His friendship as well as His parables. Reread "A Word from Peter" (page 48) and think about your own answers to the discussion questions.

Focus Verse

And the God of all grace, who called you to his eternal glory in Christ, after you have suffered a little while, will himself restore you and make you strong, firm and steadfast.

(1 Peter 5:10)

What You Will Need

- *Perfectly Flawed* DVD and DVD player, or equipment to stream the lesson-related video online
- Your Bible and *Perfectly Flawed Participant Workbook* for reference
- Copies of the contact or snack sheets filled out the previous week
- Markerboard or chart paper and markers (optional)
- Stick-on name tags and markers (optional)
- Smartphone or tablet and a portable speaker (optional)
- Various versions of the Bible for additional references or for participants who might have forgotten theirs
- YouTube video(s) cued up and ready to play

Session Outline

Welcome and Opening Prayer (5-10 minutes, depending on session length)

To create a warm, welcoming environment as the women are gathering before the session begins, consider providing coffee or other refreshments and playing worship music. If you have new participants this week who may be unknown to the group, use the name tags one more week so everyone will feel comfortable. Then, when you are ready to begin, pray the opening prayer below or offer your own.

Icebreaker (5 minutes)

Use the following icebreaker question to briefly engage the women and to help them feel comfortable with one another: Do you enjoy reading or watching movies more? What is a book or movie that you have enjoyed recently?

Video (20-25 minutes)

Next, watch the week's video segment together. Be sure to direct participants to the "Learn with Lisa: Video Viewer Guide" in the participant workbook (page 78), which they may complete as they watch the video. (Answers can be found on page 60 of this leader guide or page 232 of the participant workbook.)

Group Discussion (25-35 minutes, depending on session length)

After watching the video, choose from the questions provided below to facilitate group discussion (questions are provided for both the video and the participant workbook). For the workbook portion, you may choose to read aloud excerpts from the participant workbook—or express them in your own words; then use one or more of the questions that follow to guide your conversation.

Note that more material is provided than you will have time to include. Before the session, select what you want to cover, putting a check mark beside it in your book. Reflect on each question and make some notes in the margins to share during your discussion time. Participants will need Bibles in order to look up various supplementary scriptures.

Depending on the number of women in your group and the level of their participation, you may not have time to cover everything you have selected, and that is okay. Rather than attempting to bulldoze through, follow the Spirit's lead and be open to where the Spirit takes the conversation. Remember that your role is not to have all the answers but to encourage discussion and sharing.

- In your opinion, what qualities in Jesus did Peter see that helped him overcome his fear?
- What have you experienced that helps you overcome fear through faith in Jesus?
- In your life, how have you overcome a deep fear?
- How have you seen fear, faith, and courage work together in your life?

PARTICIPANT WORKBOOK DISCUSSION QUESTIONS

- What is something hard that you have done?
- What is something that you are afraid of?
- What stands out about the account of Peter walking on the water?
- Where do you need to keep your focus on Jesus this week?
- What is one thing that you would like your group to pray for you this week?

Deeper Conversation (15 minutes)

If your group is meeting for 90 minutes, you can choose to stay together for more discussion time or divide into groups of two or three within your small group. This time allows women to share more intimately and build connections with one another. (If breaking into smaller groups, encourage the women to break into different groups each week.) Before the session, write on a marker board or large piece of paper one or more of the questions below for groups to discuss. Give a two-minute warning before time is up so that the groups may wrap up their conversations.

Additional discussion questions for Week 2: (Participants may wish to refer to their participant workbooks. Page number references are provided beside each question.)

- What do you think that Jesus has *entrusted* you with? (page 53)
- How do you nourish your soul regularly? (page 65)
- What are some of the traditions that your family keeps? (pages 68–69)
- In what ways do you prioritize and practice forgiveness? (page 76)

WORSHIP TIME

When you sense the discussion has concluded, and especially if there is not enough time to engage in deeper, small group conversations, encourage the group take a few moments and worship the Lord who has brought you together. To guide them, play one of the YouTube videos featured this week and allow a few moments of silent reflection before you take prayer requests.

You may find that worship works well to ease your group from a deep discussion into a time of prayer.

Closing Comments and Prayer (5 minutes)

Before taking prayer requests, follow up on those voiced the previous week. Invite the women to briefly name prayer requests. As women share, write each request in your participant workbook, indicating that you will remember to pray for them during the week.

Encourage members to participate in the Closing Prayer by praying out loud for one another and the requests given. Encourage the women to volunteer to pray for specific requests, or have each woman pray for the woman on her right or left. Make sure name tags are visible so that group members do not feel awkward if they don't remember names well.

Close by leading the group in prayer, using the written prayer below, or offer a closing prayer yourself. Afterward, remind women to pray for one another throughout the week, and text at least one member this week to remind her you are praying for her, and that God will help her through the storms she faces.

CLOSING PRAYER

Father, we once again praise Your name and give thanks for the gift of this time together for fellowship and growth. Thank You for calling us each to Yourself and thank You for Your presence with us in the storms. Help us keep our eyes on You and not the situation around us. Thank You for Your work in our lives. Amen.

Perfectly FLAWED and HOPEFUL

(Peter Learned from Jesus)

Notes

_____

_____

_____

_____

_____

_____

_____

_____

_____

_____

_____

Leader Preparation (Before the Session)

Overview

This week, we looked at selected verses from the life of Peter, including selections from his epistles (letters to the early followers of Jesus), Acts, and the Gospels. This week focused on how the teachings Peter learned changed his life and his relationships with others, including Jesus. His life changed forever. He would never again be a Galilean fisherman, even though his life on the sea taught him much he would use later in his life and ministry. He was still a work in process, even after years of following Jesus, but he was growing into a future leader after the Resurrection and Pentecost. The lesson also focused on how Jesus focused on preparing Peter to lead those around him and to direct them away from the evil that abounds in this world. As they journeyed toward the inevitable end of Jesus's life, He knew Peter's faith would be tested and purified. Everything the disciples thought they knew about Jesus would be turned upside down. Reread "A Word from Peter" (page 82) and think about your own answers to the discussion questions.

Focus Verse

Praise be to the God and Father of our Lord Jesus Christ! In his great mercy he has given us new birth into a living hope through the resurrection of Jesus Christ from the dead.

(1 Peter 1:3)

What You Will Need

- *Perfectly Flawed* DVD and DVD player, or equipment to stream the lesson-related video online
- Your Bible and *Perfectly Flawed Participant Workbook* for reference
- Copies of the contact or snack sheets filled out the previous week
- Markerboard or chart paper and markers (optional)
- Stick-on name tags and markers (optional)
- Smartphone or tablet and a portable speaker (optional)
- Various versions of the Bible for additional references or for participants who might have forgotten theirs
- YouTube video(s) cued up and ready to play

Session Outline

Welcome and Opening Prayer (5-10 minutes, depending on session length)

To create a warm, welcoming environment as the women are gathering before the session begins, consider providing coffee or other refreshments and playing worship music. If you have new participants this week who may be unknown to the group, use the name tags one more week so everyone will feel comfortable. Then, when you are ready to begin, pray the opening prayer below or offer your own.

OPENING PRAYER

Lord, we thank You for the gift of spending another week in Your Word. We thank You for the community we share and the ability to do life together. Open our hearts to the lessons of this study and allow us to see how we can learn from Peter's life—both his triumphs and his mistakes. We ask that You use this study to help us grow closer to You and Your Son, Jesus. Amen.

Icebreaker (5 minutes)

Use the following icebreaker question to briefly engage the women and to help them feel comfortable with one another: How do you cope with work, housecleaning, or another required task when you are just *not* in the mood to tackle it?

Video (20-25 minutes)

Next, watch the week's video segment together. Be sure to direct participants to the "Learn with Lisa: Video Viewer Guide" in the participant workbook (page 114), which they may complete as they watch the video. (Answers can be found on page 60 of this leader guide or page 232 of the participant workbook.)

Group Discussion (25-35 minutes, depending on session length)

After watching the video, choose from the questions provided below to facilitate group discussion (questions are provided for both the video and the participant workbook). For the workbook portion, you may choose to read aloud excerpts from the participant workbook—or express them in your own words; then use one or more of the questions that follow to guide your conversation.

Note that more material is provided than you will have time to include. Before the session, select what you want to cover, putting a check mark beside it in your book. Reflect on each question and make some notes in the margins to share during your discussion time. Participants will need Bibles in order to look up various supplementary scriptures.

Depending on the number of women in your group and the level of their participation, you may not have time to cover everything you have selected, and that is okay. Rather than attempting to bulldoze through, follow the Spirit's lead and be open to where the Spirit takes the conversation. Remember that your role is not to have all the answers but to encourage discussion and sharing.

VIDEO DISCUSSION QUESTIONS

- Have you ever experienced the kind of discomfort the disciples must have felt at Caesarea Philippi? Why were you wary?
- Why do you think Jesus chose this place to ask His disciples, "Who do you say I am?"
- When people ask about why you believe in Jesus, what do you tell them?
- In what ways does your faith in Jesus provide hope in your life?

PARTICIPANT WORKBOOK DISCUSSION QUESTIONS

- What is your faith background?
- When did you first come to know Jesus?
- What stands out to you about the account of Peter proclaiming Jesus to be the Messiah in Caesarea Philippi?
- Who in your life needs to know the truth of who Jesus is?
- What is one thing that you would like your group to pray for you this week?

Deeper Conversation (15 minutes)

If your group is meeting for 90 minutes, you can choose to stay together for more discussion time or divide into groups of two or three within your small group. This time allows women to share more intimately and build connections with one another. (If breaking into smaller groups, encourage the women to break into different groups each week.) Before the session, write on a markerboard or large piece of paper one or more of the questions below for groups to discuss. Give a two-minute warning before time is up so that the groups may wrap up their conversations.

Additional discussion questions for Week 3: (Participants may wish to refer to their participant workbooks. Page number references are provided beside each question.)

- What is one of your flaws that you would like to change? How have you asked Jesus to help reshape your flaw? (page 83)
- In what way does our world need the power of God's transformation? (page 94)
- What are some skills or experiences from your past that you haven't used in a while? (page 98) How could you use those now in acting on your faith and helping others?
- What are some of the distractions you are facing right now? (page 109) How do you think this study can help with those?

When you sense the discussion has concluded, and especially if there is not enough time to engage in deeper, small group conversations, encourage the group take a few moments and worship the Lord who has brought you together. To guide them, play one of the YouTube videos featured this week and allow a few moments of silent reflection before you take prayer requests. You may find that worship works well to ease your group from deep discussion into a time of prayer.

Closing Comments and Prayer (5 minutes)

Before taking prayer requests, follow up on those voiced the previous two weeks. Find out how God is moving. (This will encourage women who might think God doesn't answer their prayers.) Invite the women to briefly name prayer requests. As women share, write each request in your participant workbook, indicating that you will remember to pray for them during the week.

Encourage members to participate in the Closing Prayer by praying out loud for one another and the requests given. Encourage a woman to pray for the specific needs highlighted by the other members in the group. Or enlist different women to pray for one of the prayer requests, making sure they know which request they are offering to God.

Close by leading the group in prayer, using the written prayer below, or offer a closing prayer yourself. Afterward, remind women to pray for one another throughout the week, and text at least one member this week to remind her you are praying for her, and that God will help her to stay focused on Him.

CLOSING PRAYER

Father, we praise You because You are the sovereign King over the universe. All authorities and powers, seen and unseen, bow at the mention of Your name. Thank You for being sovereign over our lives because we can trust You with whatever lies ahead. You are good and what You do is good. Allow us to stay focused on You this week. In the name of Jesus, our Bright and Morning Star. Amen.

Perfectly FLAWED and HUMBLE

(Peter Denied Jesus)

Notes

_____

_____

_____

_____

_____

_____

_____

_____

_____

_____

_____

Leader Preparation (Before the Session)

Overview

This week, we looked at selected verses from the life of Peter, including selections from his epistles, Acts, and the Gospels. This week focused on Peter's denial of Jesus and the sorrow and anguish he experienced as a result. Like many believers today, Peter's flaws were exposed when he least expected. But Jesus never expected him—nor us—to be perfect. He knows and understands our flaws and can guide us through them, in the same way He guided Peter through repentance and forgiveness. As a fisherman repairs nets, Jesus can heal our hearts. The lesson also focused on how our faith can anchor us and help us navigate the trials of life, as well as the importance of demonstrating compassion for others—even when they betray us. Reread "A Word from Peter" (page 118) and think about your own answers to the discussion questions.

Focus Verse

Humble yourselves, therefore, under God's mighty hand, that he may lift you up in due time. Cast all your anxiety on him because he cares for you.

(1 Peter 5:6-7)

What You Will Need

- *Perfectly Flawed* DVD and DVD player or equipment to stream the lesson-related video online
- Your Bible and *Perfectly Flawed Participant Workbook* for reference
- Copies of the contact or snack sheets filled out the previous week
- Markerboard or chart paper and markers (optional)
- Stick-on name tags and markers (optional)
- Smartphone or tablet and a portable speaker (optional)
- Various versions of the Bible for additional references or for participants who might have forgotten theirs
- YouTube video(s) cued up and ready to play

Session Outline

Welcome and Opening Prayer (5-10 minutes, depending on session length)

To create a warm, welcoming environment as the women are gathering before the session begins, consider providing coffee or other refreshments and playing worship music. Continue to use name tags if you have a large group and women have not had the opportunity to meet everyone. When you are ready to begin, pray the opening prayer below or offer your own.

Our Lord and God, we thank You for Your unfailing, unfaltering, unending love for us. Thank You that Your mercies are new every morning, that You throw our sin into the heart of the sea and remember them no more. Spirit, we invite You into this space, this time with one another. Move in our hearts, direct our conversations, and change our thoughts. We want to be people who can be called seekers of Your heart. In Your name we pray. Amen.

Icebreaker (5 minutes)

Use the following icebreaker question to briefly engage the women and to help them feel comfortable with one another: Do you enjoy cooking or eating out more? What are some of your favorite foods?

Video (20-25 minutes)

Next, watch the week's video segment together. Be sure to direct participants to the "Learn with Lisa: Video Viewer Guide" in the participant workbook (page 152), which they may complete as they watch the video. (Answers can be found on page 60 of this leader guide or page 232 of the participant workbook.)

Group Discussion (25-35 minutes, depending on session length)

After watching the video, choose from the questions provided below to facilitate group discussion (questions are provided for both the video and the participant workbook). For the workbook portion, you may choose to read aloud excerpts from the participant workbook—or express them in your own words; then use one or more of the questions that follow to guide your conversation.

Note that more material is provided than you will have time to include. Before the session, select what you want to cover, putting a check mark beside it in your book. Reflect on each question and make some notes in the margins to share during your discussion time. Participants will need Bibles in order to look up various supplementary scriptures.

Depending on the number of women in your group and the level of their participation, you may not have time to cover everything you have selected, and that is okay. Rather than attempting to bulldoze through, follow the Spirit's lead and be open to where the Spirit takes the conversation. Remember that your role is not to have all the answers but to encourage discussion and sharing.

- Have you ever felt too flawed or sinful to be forgiven? How does it feel to be forgiven?
- Do you sometimes struggle to serve others, even if you feel called to do so? In what ways does your faith in Jesus help you with that struggle?
- Have you ever watched events in your life go "sideways"? How did your trust in Jesus help you in that circumstance?
- In what ways do you feel Jesus has restored you, either mentally, emotionally, physically, or spiritually, or all of these?
- How do you think Peter felt after being forgiven? How do you think his betrayal of Jesus—and his restoration—impacted Peter's ministry?

Participant Workbook Discussion Questions

- Who is someone who has betrayed you?
- Why do you think that betrayal is so hard to recover from?
- What stands out to you about the account of how Jesus restored Peter?
- What are some ways that you have worked through the process of forgiveness?
- What is one thing that you would like your group to pray for you this week?

Deeper Conversation (15 minutes)

If your group is meeting for 90 minutes, you can choose to stay together for more discussion time or divide into groups of two or three within your small group. This time allows women to share more intimately and build connections with one another. (If breaking into smaller groups, encourage the women to break into different groups each week.) Before the session, write on a markerboard or large piece of paper one or more of the questions below for groups to discuss. Give a two-minute warning before time is up so that the groups may wrap up their conversations.

Additional discussion questions for Week 4: (Participants may wish to refer to their participant workbooks. Page number references are provided beside each question.)

- Can you think of a time when you have questioned the goodness of God? (page 121)
- What are some of your favorite attributes of your friends? (page 127)

- Where do you feel called today to persevere despite being squeezed like an olive? (page 134)
- Can you think of a time that you were truly surprised by something good? (page 144)

When you sense the discussion has concluded, and especially if there is not enough time to engage in deeper, small group conversations, encourage the group to take a few moments and worship the Lord who has brought you together. To guide them, play one of the YouTube videos featured this week and allow a few moments of silent reflection before you take prayer requests. You may find that worship works well to ease your group from a deep discussion into a time of prayer.

Closing Comments and Prayer (5 minutes)

Before taking prayer requests, follow up on those voiced the previous weeks. Find out how God is moving. (This will encourage women who might think God doesn't answer their prayers.) Invite the women to briefly name prayer requests. As women share, write each request in your participant workbook, indicating that you will remember to pray for them during the week.

For the closing prayer time, allow participants to voice their prayer requests. After each one, invite other women in the group to volunteer to pray for that specific request. Repeat this process as needed for additional requests. Invite one person to open the time of prayer and explain you will close in prayer. Use the written prayer below or offer a closing prayer yourself. Afterward, remind women to pray for one another throughout the week, and text at least one member this week to remind her you are praying for her, and that God freely forgives and restores us.

CLOSING PRAYER

Jesus, thank You for forgiveness that flows freely to us because of Your sacrificial death for our sin. Thank You that in You there is full redemption and restoration, and that You don't leave us even when we stray from You. Where we feel shame or regret from past mistakes, remind us that You see us as Your beloved daughters. Amen.

If your group would like to plan a service project to serve together, this week is a good time to choose a project.

Perfectly FLAWED and EMPOWERED

(Peter Preached Jesus)

Notes

Leader Preparation (Before the Session)

Overview

This week, we looked at selected verses from the life of Peter, including selections from his epistles, Acts, and the Gospels. This lesson focused on the spread of the gospel and the increase in Peter's strength and confidence in proclaiming the word of God. He had survived his betrayal of Jesus, mourned the Crucifixion, and celebrated the Resurrection. Jesus had restored Peter, and he had emerged a solid and assured leader among the disciples. As he and John went forth to worship and show others the wonders of God, they were often "interrupted" by the Lord to go into a different direction, demonstrating that all of us need to remain open to wherever God leads us, always standing strong in our faith. Reread "A Word from Peter" (page 156) and think about your own answers to the discussion questions.

Focus Verse

His divine power has given us everything we need for a godly life through our knowledge of him who called us by his own glory and goodness.

(2 Peter 1:3)

What You Will Need

- *Perfectly Flawed* DVD and DVD player, or equipment to stream the lesson-related video online
- Your Bible and *Perfectly Flawed Participant Workbook* for reference
- Copies of the contact or snack sheets filled out the previous week
- Markerboard or chart paper and markers (optional)
- Smartphone or tablet and a portable speaker (optional)
- Various versions of the Bible for additional references or for participants who might have forgotten theirs
- YouTube video(s) cued up and ready to play

Session Outline

Welcome and Opening Prayer (5-10 minutes, depending on session length)

To create a warm, welcoming environment as the women are gathering before the session begins, consider providing coffee or other refreshments and playing worship music. If you have new participants this week who may be unknown to the group, use the name tags one more week so everyone will feel comfortable. Then, when you are ready to begin, pray the opening prayer below or offer your own.

Lord, we thank You for this gathering of believers who seek to follow You just as Peter did, with our whole hearts and lives. Help us see that just as You led Peter, forgave him, and helped him grow into a confident leader, so You can show us how to grow in our relationship with You, finding strength in your wisdom and guidance. Amen.

Icebreaker (5 minutes)

Use the following icebreaker question to briefly engage the women and to help them feel comfortable with one another: what is a hobby that you think would be fun to learn and participate in doing?

Video (20-25 minutes)

Next, watch the week's video segment together. Be sure to direct participants to the "Learn with Lisa: Video Viewer Guide" in the participant workbook (page 190), which they may complete as they watch the video. (Answers can be found on page 60 of this leader guide or page 232 of the participant workbook.)

Group Discussion (25-35 minutes, depending on session length)

After watching the video, choose from the questions provided below to facilitate group discussion (questions are provided for both the video and the participant workbook). For the workbook portion, you may choose to read aloud excerpts from the participant workbook—or express them in your own words; then use one or more of the questions that follow to guide your conversation.

Note that more material is provided than you will have time to include. Before the session, select what you want to cover, putting a check mark beside it in your book. Reflect on each question and make some notes in the margins to share during your discussion time. Participants will need Bibles in order to look up various supplementary scriptures.

Depending on the number of women in your group and the level of their participation, you may not have time to cover everything you have selected, and that is okay. Rather than attempting to bulldoze through, follow the Spirit's lead and be open to where the Spirit takes the conversation. Remember that your role is not to have all the answers but to encourage discussion and sharing.

- Do you sometimes find yourself doubting that God will ever answer your prayers? How do you deal with that doubt?
- What prayers have you seen answered after months—if not years—of waiting?
- What are some gifts God has given you?
- How do you know the Holy Spirit is moving in your life?

PARTICIPANT WORKBOOK DISCUSSION QUESTIONS

- Who are some of the people in your life who have been spiritually influential?
- What is one of your favorite podcasts, books, apps, or other spiritual resource?
- What stands out to you about the account of Peter and the Pentecost?
- In what ways would you like to invite the Holy Spirit to be active in your life?
- What is one thing that you would like your group to pray for you this week?

Deeper Conversation (15 minutes)

If your group is meeting for 90 minutes, you can choose to stay together for more discussion time or divide into groups of two or three within your small group. This time allows women to share more intimately and build connections with one another. (If breaking into smaller groups, encourage the women to break into different groups each week.) Before the session, write on a markerboard or large piece of paper one or more of the questions below for groups to discuss. Give a two-minute warning before time is up so that the groups may wrap up their conversations.

Additional discussion questions for Week 5: (Participants may wish to refer to their participant workbooks. Page number references are provided beside each question.)

- What do you need for God to turn beautiful in your life? (page 161)
- How is the experience of praying in a group different for you than praying alone? (page 171)
- When have you lived in the shadows or experienced darkness? (page 186) Did your faith help during that time, or did you feel alone, without the presence of God?
- Where do you need to take refuge today in the shadow of the wings of the Almighty? (page 186)

Allow time for this to happen after the discussion period. It can be used to bring the groups back together (if they have broken into small groups) or bring an end to a central discussion. Once you feel the discussion has concluded, and especially if there is not enough time to engage in deeper small group conversations, suggest that the group take a few moments and worship the Lord who has brought you together. Play one of the YouTube videos featured this week and allow a few moments of reflection before beginning the closing prayer requests. You may find that this option works well to ease your group from an intense discussion into a time of prayer requests.

Closing Comments and Prayer (5 minutes)

Before taking prayer requests, follow up on those voiced during the previous weeks. Find out how God is moving. (This will encourage women who might think God doesn't answer their prayers.) Invite the women to briefly name prayer requests. As women share, write each request in your participant workbook, indicating that you will remember to pray for them during the week.

For the Closing Prayer, explain that you will read out each request mentioned; you will pause for a moment of silence so women can pray. Repeat this process for each prayer request, pausing to allow women to intercede for their fellow participants. Close the prayer time by praying aloud, using the one below or voicing your own. After the prayer, remind the women to pray for one another throughout the week, and text at least one member a week to remind them of your prayer and God's love.

Closing Prayer

Our great Redeemer, we thank You for making broken places in our lives beautiful again. Thank You that our failures are not final, and that You are good and what You do is good. When we are faced with persecution for our faith or walk through a season of darkness, give us the grace to sense Your Spirit as our companion and our comfort. Remind us that You promised that You would never leave us or forsake us. We lean into You and trust You because You are trustworthy. Amen.

Perfectly FLAWED and FAITHFUL

(Peter Persisted for Jesus)

Notes

_____

_____

_____

_____

_____

_____

_____

_____

_____

_____

_____

Leader Preparation (Before the Session)

Remember as you lead this discussion that the session will proceed in a slightly different way than the others. This concluding session may be more emotional for some of the participants as they prepare to say farewell to the group and the study. Try to cut a few minutes off each section of the discussion and allow time for more sharing. If you have not provided tissues before, have some handy.

Overview

This week, we looked at selected verses from the life of Peter, including selections from his epistles, Acts, and the Gospels. This week focused on Peter's persistence in the face of the obstacles he and the other disciples faced as they sought to share the words of Jesus. As with all believers, the apostles faced naysayers and doubters, but they stayed firm in the face of those who would wish to harm them. The anchor for them through all of this—as it is for us—is Jesus, who wanted to bring all God's children into the fold. Today, the church needs to continue and live out all that Jesus and the ministries of Peter and the others have taught us, persisting in reaching out and welcoming everyone. Reread "A Word from Peter" (page 194) and think about your own answers to the discussion questions.

Focus Verse

Each of you should use whatever gift you have received to serve others, as faithful stewards of God's grace in its various forms.

(1 Peter 4:10)

What You Will Need

- *Perfectly Flawed* DVD and DVD player, or equipment to stream the lesson-related video online
- Your Bible and *Perfectly Flawed* Participant Workbook for reference
- Copies of the contact or snack sheets filled out the previous week
- Markerboard or chart paper and markers (optional)
- Stick-on name tags and markers (optional)
- Smartphone or tablet and a portable speaker (optional)
- Various versions of the Bible for additional references or for participants who might have forgotten theirs
- YouTube video(s) cued up and ready to play

Session Outline

Welcome and Opening Prayer (5-10 minutes, depending on session length)

For this last session, bring unique snacks to the table (such as a cake) to create an atmosphere of joy and celebration as well as study. Use your own creativity for this, whether it's food, décor, or special music for the background during these few minutes of gathering. Allow for a little fellowship but remember to honor women's time and involvement. Start on time and pray the opening prayer that is provided or offer your own.

OPENING PRAYER

Good and gracious God, thank You for the opportunity to gather for this Bible study. Thank You for Your living Word, sharper than any two-edged sword, that is able to guide, comfort, challenge, encourage, and draw us closer to You. As we learn, discuss, and share together, may our conversation bring glory to You and lead to changed lives. Amen.

Icebreaker (5 minutes)

Use the following icebreaker question to briefly engage the women and to help them feel comfortable with one another: what is an embarrassing moment that you have had to navigate?

Video (20-25 minutes)

Next, watch the week's video segment together. Be sure to direct participants to the "Learn with Lisa: Video Viewer Guide" in the participant workbook (page 226), which they may complete as they watch the video. (Answers can be found on page 60 of this leader guide or page 232 of the participant workbook.)

Group Discussion (25-35 minutes, depending on session length)

After watching the video, choose from the questions provided below to facilitate group discussion (questions are provided for both the video and the participant workbook). For the workbook portion, you may choose to read aloud excerpts from the participant workbook—or express them in your own words; then use one or more of the questions that follow to guide your conversation.

Note that more material is provided than you will have time to include. Before the session, select what you want to cover, putting a check mark beside it in your book. Reflect on each question and make some notes in the margins to share during your discussion time. Participants will need Bibles in order to look up various supplementary scriptures.

Depending on the number of women in your group and the level of their participation, you may not have time to cover everything you have selected, and that is okay. Rather than attempting to bulldoze through, follow the Spirit's lead and be open to where the Spirit takes the conversation. Remember that your role is not to have all the answers but to encourage discussion and sharing.

Video Discussion Questions

- If you are a "type A" personality, in what ways do you seek to make things in your life "perfect"?
- What flaws in yourself do you conceal from your friends or church? Do you think they will make you less lovable in their eyes? Explain.
- In what ways could counting your blessings give you a better perspective when you get caught up in what is going wrong in your life?
- How can you rely on Jesus to see you through the rougher times in your life?
- How does the love of Jesus for you—and He does love you—help you see yourself in a different light?

Participant Workbook Discussion Questions

- Read Acts 9:32-43. What stands out to you about the account of Peter with Aeneas and Dorcas (Tabitha)?
- Where have you seen Jesus be your strength when you felt weak?
- What will you remember most about Peter and his journey with Jesus from this study?
- How can you let your flaws be used by God to reveal His strength, power, and glory?
- What is one of the most helpful things God has revealed to you during this six-week study?

Deeper Conversation (15 minutes)

If your group is meeting for 90 minutes, you can choose to stay together for more discussion time or divide into groups of two or three within your small group. This time allows women to share more intimately and build connections with one another. (If breaking into smaller groups, encourage the women to break into different groups each week.) Before the session, write on a marker board or large piece of paper one or more of the questions below for groups to discuss. Give a two-minute warning before time is up so that the groups may wrap up their conversations.

Additional discussion questions for Week 6: (Participants may wish to refer to their participant workbooks. Page number references are provided beside each question.)

- What are some relationships that have helped you in a positive way to challenge stereotypes and culture? (page 195)
- Can you think of a time when God showed up for you in a way you never expected? (page 204)
- Have you ever lost a friend to conflict that you could not resolve? (page 206)
- How has God used this study on Peter to grow your faith? (page 224)

WORSHIP TIME

When you sense the discussion has concluded, and especially if there is not enough time to engage in deeper, small group conversations, encourage the group take a few moments and worship the Lord who has brought you together. To guide them, play one of the YouTube videos featured this week and allow a few moments of silent reflection before you take prayer requests. You may find that worship works well to ease your group from a deep discussion into a time of prayer.

A Final Word and Closing Prayer (5-10 minutes)

As you wrap up today's discussion and before closing the study with prayer, read the "Final Word" verses listed below.

A FINAL WORD FROM PETER

His divine power has given us everything we need for a godly life through our knowledge of him who called us by his own glory and goodness. Through these he has given us his very great and precious promises, so that through them you may participate in the divine nature, having escaped the corruption in the world caused by evil desires.

For this very reason, make every effort to add to your faith goodness; and to goodness, knowledge; and to knowledge, self-control; and to self-control, perseverance; and to perseverance, godliness; and to godliness, mutual affection; and to mutual affection, love. For if you possess these qualities in increasing measure, they will keep you from being ineffective and unproductive in your knowledge of our Lord Jesus Christ.

(2 Peter 1:3-8)

But grow in the grace and knowledge of our Lord and Savior Jesus Christ. To Him be glory both now and forever. Amen.

(2 Peter 3:18)

And I tell you that you are Peter, and on this rock I will build my church, and the gates of Hades will not overcome it.

(Matthew 16:18)

Just before prayer, encourage women to think about the questions below as they reflect on this Bible study. Encourage them to celebrate, share, and build upon what the study has meant to them:

- What prayers have been answered?
- Where has God provided direction on next steps?
- Where have you seen God be strong when you felt weak?
- What friendships have been built?
- How have you grown in your faith?
- How has your relationship with Jesus been impacted through the journey with Peter?

Closing Comments and Prayer (5 minutes)

Before taking prayer requests, follow up on those voiced during the previous weeks. Find out how God is moving. (This will encourage women who might think God doesn't answer their prayers.) Invite the women to briefly name prayer requests. As women share, write each request in your participant workbook, indicating that you will remember to pray for them during the week.

Open the prayer time by thanking God for bringing the group together, for your time together, and for the women's openness to Him and one another. Ask God to keep their hearts open to hearing more from Him as they go forth. Pray for each woman, thanking Him for a specific way each one has blessed you. Pray for any specific prayer requests each woman may have voiced and pray a word of blessing over each one.

After the prayer, remind the women to pray for one another throughout the week and text each woman this week to remind them of your prayers and God's deep, unfailing love for them.

Allow time for the participants to exchange their goodbyes or move into a time of celebration together!

Let's Celebrate!

There are lots of different ways that you could have a celebration to conclude your study. Here are some ideas. You can brainstorm more with your team:

- Host a potluck meal together (everyone brings a dish to share).
- Invite the group to a dessert and coffee reception.
- To serve others, plan a shower for an expectant mom (or something similar).
- Leaders could bring a gift for each group member.
- Allow for an extended time of closing prayer and worship to celebrate.
- Invite members to all go out to lunch or dinner together.
- Cater in a meal to share together.
- Host a tea party.
- Share Communion together.
- Promote your next Bible study and have sign-ups available to keep the momentum going.

Thank you for leading a group!

I'D LOVE TO HEAR FROM YOU!

I love to hear the stories of God's transforming power. What has God done in your group? You can easily share a story that may used to bless, encourage, or minister to someone else. Upload the story at **lisatoney.com/perfectlyflawedstories**.

Please stay in touch on Instagram and Facebook:

LisaToneyLife   LisaToneyLife

Take a photo with your book or small group and post it with these hashtags to share in the joy of our *Perfectly Flawed* community, which is leaning into the transformative power of Jesus to turn our weaknesses into strengths for His glory.

#peterrocks #perfectlyflawed

Video Viewer Guide: *Answers*

Week 1

disrupt

love | FISH

depth | emptiness |

answer

Jesus

love | disrupts | hope

right relationships

LIVING HOPE

trade | strengths

sin

abundance | emptiness

love | disrupts | hope

Week 2

near | fear

let go | hold on

taking action

paralyzes | mobilizes

towards | meets

haze | gaze

with

Week 3

Pantheism

Man

God

living hope

Anointed One

Anointed One

endure

enough

Week 4

compassion

identity

caved

risen | dead

need

imperfections | used

wastes | pain

abundance

Week 5

ALIVE

each | individually

new harvest

soul

waiting | working

remain

asking | trusting

faithful

Week 6

hide | expose

perfection | direction

right | wrong

strength

compassion | action

goodness

LEARN
with
LISA

Group Roster

Name	Email Address	Phone Number

Name	Email Address	Phone Number

Watch videos based on *Perfectly Flawed: God Transforms Our Weaknesses into Strengths*
with Lisa Toney
through Amplify Media.

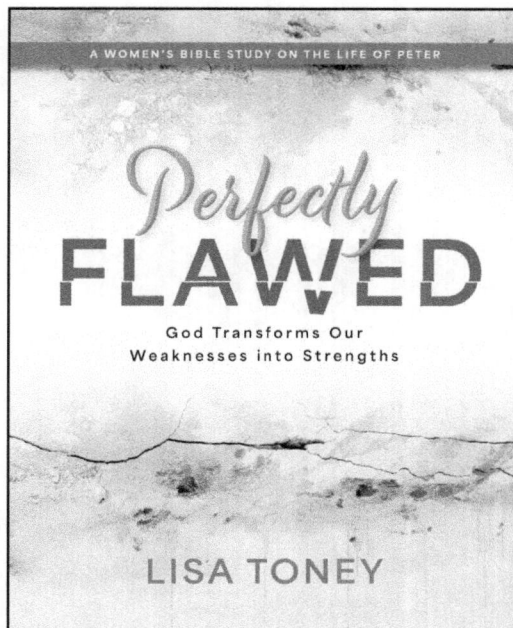

Amplify Media is a multimedia platform that delivers high-quality, searchable content with an emphasis on Wesleyan perspectives for churchwide, group, or individual use on any device at any time. In a world of sometimes overwhelming choices, Amplify gives church leaders and congregants media capabilities that are contemporary, relevant, effective, and, most important, affordable and sustainable.

With *Amplify Media* church leaders can:

- Provide a reliable source of Christian content through a Wesleyan lens for teaching, training, and inspiration in a customizable library
- Deliver their own preaching and worship content in a way the congregation knows and appreciates
- Build the church's capacity to innovate with engaging content and accessible technology
- Equip the congregation to better understand the Bible and its application
- Deepen discipleship beyond the church walls

⅄ AMPLIFY. MEDIA

Ask your group leader or pastor about Amplify Media
and sign up today at www.AmplifyMedia.com.

Printed in the USA
CPSIA information can be obtained
at www.ICGtesting.com
LVHW080823051224
797945LV00002B/7